Watermark

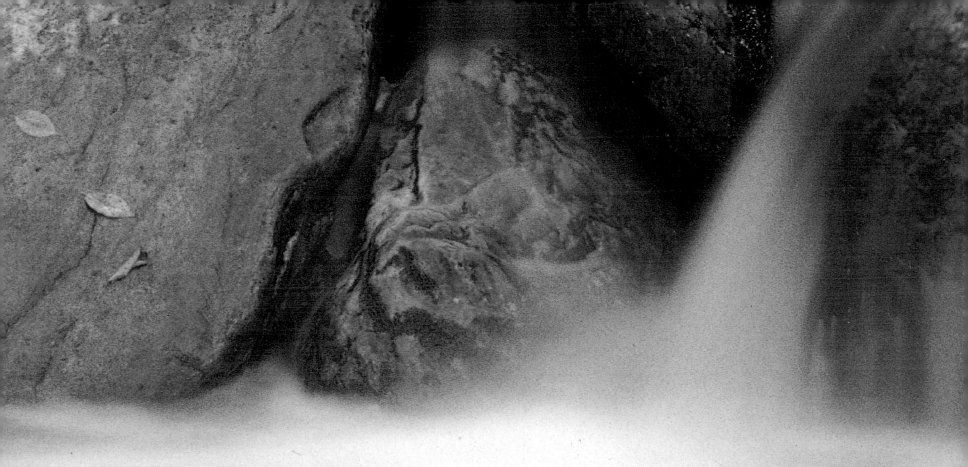

Watermark

GRANT MCCLINTOCK AND MIKE CROCKETT

THE LYONS PRESS   NEW YORK

The rivers of the East carry more than
salmon and dappled brook trout, more than
maple leaves in autumn and rhododendron
petals in summer. They carry our history
and flow with our hopes into the future.
These rivers have etched a watermark
across the land—a trace of the past pulled
forward. The mark is subtle but the sense of
it is strong. It reminds us that we are not
the first here nor will we be the last.

McClintock, Grant.
    Watermark / Grant McClintock and Mike Crockett.
            p.   cm.
    ISBN 1–55821–779–7
    1. Fly fishing — Pictorial works. 2. Fly fishing — East (U.S.) —
Pictorial works. 3. Fly fishing — Canada, Eastern — Pictorial works.
    I. Crockett, Mike.   II. Title.
    SH4G4.UGM35   1998
    799. 1'755—dc21   98-26268
                                                        CIP

THE LYONS PRESS

31 WEST TWENTY-FIRST STREET
NEW YORK, NEW YORK 10010
1-800-836-0510
FAX 212.929.1836

DESIGNED BY CAROL HARALSON

ALL PHOTOGRAPHS BY GRANT MCCLINTOCK

PRINTED IN HONG KONG

10 9 8 7 6 5 4 3 2 1

ISBN 1-55821-779-7

Introduction

NICK LYONS

WATERMARK is a rich and revealing sequel to *Flywater,* that miraculous book that celebrated the majestic waters and spaces of the American West. But it is a continuation in a new key. For while the stunning photography of Grant McClintock remains a happy constant, the images that his camera records have shifted radically. *Watermark* celebrates vastly different county—from the Southeast on up to the great rivers of Pennsylvania, New York, and Maine, and finally to the Atlantic salmon waters of Canada, especially the Margaree, a place so compelling that Grant can end this stunning book by saying simply, "I could live there."

The images in *Watermark* are more intimate, the fly fishing that animates the book more familiar, at least to my eastern eyes. There are more people here and towns and bridges, for the East has been more lived in, and by larger numbers of people, for much longer; it has been written about much more and it has more history. Though it is for the most part less spectacular, though the rivers are more crowded and the fish smaller, it can be compelling in its own ways—and its character is chiefly what Grant's camera seeks to uncover.

But there is another, and very special difference between *Flywater* and *Watermark.* There have been any number of fine books by easterners and midwesterners who—wide-eyed—have discovered the West. This is a rare, even unique, book by westerners looking to discover what for many is the all-too-discovered East—the nature of those who fish it, the size of the fish, the cut of the rivers, the interconnection between the worlds of rivers and the world that surround them, for fishing, especially fly fishing, is never a disembodied activity, sufficient to the physical activity itself, but a passion inextricably linked to the fish, the people, the rivers, and the surrounding land. The horizons here may "appear limited," as Mike Crockett says in his prefatory essay, but "to eastern eyes, these same horizons are close at hand, familiar, and touchable." Chiefly, *Watermark* is a search, an exploration undertaken by passionate fly fishers. And the same spirit that animated *Flywater*—an insatiable curiosity, an abiding love of fly fishing (which miraculously seems to have contributed to Mike's continuing triumph over cancer), and a great passion to see, experience, and record.

We get memorable photographs of Avery Creek in North Carolina, the Tallulah River in Georgia, the Middle Prong Little

River in Tennessee, and Cascades Creek in Virginia, a lovely piece of water, pleated with waterfalls. These waters are home to small, native Appalachian brookies, bright black and red and white, like little live jewels, and they are waters deep in a part of the world noted more for its quail hunting and cotton and heat than trout fishing.

Further north, Grant's lens explores the famed Beaverkill and Willowemoc, while Fen Montaigne interviews two heirs to and participants in the long Catskill tradition, Ed Van Put and Joan Wulff, probing their relationship to the country and the fishing, who they are and why they chose to live where they do.

Penns Creek, the LeTort, the Yellow Breeches; the West Branch of the Ausable, the Saranac, the Boquet—and then on to the great salmon rivers, the Miramichi, the Bonaventure, the Matapédia, the Cascapédia, and finally the Margaree. It is the last, in Cape Breton, that provides the most abiding connection—far from Grant's Oklahoma, one that "at once humbles the ego and expands the soul."

This is a memorable and intensely evocative book—a celebration of eastern places and a deep celebration of the special joys of fly fishing. If you know *Flywater* well, *Watermark* brings East and West into an especially meaningful relationship—at a time when, somehow, I hear more and more grumbling that wants to tear them apart. The photography is stunning, capturing the special world and people of an older place that is new to this photographer's lens. And you can feel the newness to Grant and Mike, their eagerness to explore and discover—from the faces of New Englanders to the pristine beauty of the Margaree Valley. *Watermark* finds and records a memorable world I thought I knew, a world that many easterners along with westerners have never seen so clearly and evocatively. I love this book and think fly fishers across the country will love it too.

NEW YORK CITY
APRIL 1998

Willowemoc River, New York

The First Best Place

MIKE CROCKETT

LAST SPRING, as Grant McClintock and I began discussing another photo-essay project, covering the trout and salmon streams of the eastern United States and Canada, it occurred to me that I knew next to nothing about fishing in the East. Westerners tend to assume that the best in fly fishing is here at home. Few of us take the opportunity to find out what the sport is about on the side of the country where American fly fishing was born. The closest most westerners get to eastern fly fishing is bumping into New Yorkers on the Bighorn or the Madison.

As a boy from Oklahoma who never traveled in the East until well into adulthood, I grew up somewhat in awe of the social and artistic brilliance of the East and easterners. New York was a glamorous foreign city I knew only from the movies. The West was pretty much the same, except John Wayne replaced Fred Astaire. I was simply a kid living in small-town middle America.

In the last few years, first moving from Oklahoma to Colorado and then traveling to Montana, Idaho, and other western fishing destinations, I have finally begun to consider myself a westerner. As my tenure as a western fly fisherman has grown, I became more interested in our sport's history, especially its roots in this country. Of course, I knew fly fishing began in the East, and I was familiar with the names of the more famous rivers, but after that my knowledge fell off quickly. So I went to the books. I soon learned that nobody seems to know who the first American fly fisherman was, but that the roots of the modern sport in our country lay in the Catskills in the 19th century, especially after 1851, when the Erie Railroad along the Delaware improved access for New Yorkers to streams like the Beaverkill and the Willowemoc. Reading further of some of the strange characters who were notables of the sport in early America, I began to be persuaded that my research time could be more pleasurably spent exploring the actual trout streams they had fished. For a confirmed fishhead, always enthralled with the idea of stepping into a stream for the first time, the proposal for a fly fishing project based in the East was not an offer to be refused.

The questions had been in mind for years: "How do those old boys in the East dress when they go fishing? Are they a bunch of dry-fly snobs? What size fish do they catch? What's it look like back there? How big are the streams? What about access? Is it crowded? What kind of flies do they use?"

For readers already familiar with the rivers of the West, a glance through the pages of *Watermark* will reveal a few of the answers to these questions. Perhaps the most common question (at least from a certain moon-eyed group of anglers) is about the size of the fish. Of course, philosophically, size doesn't matter. In the true spirit of fly fishing for trout, the angler in pursuit of the rare double-digit native brookie in the Blue Ridge Mountains is doing exactly the same thing as the steelheader who goes after the twenty-pound sea-run rainbow in the coastal streams of the Pacific Northwest. With equipment matched to the task, the theory goes, the mature angler (one who has completed the cycle of "catch any fish, catch many fish, catch a huge fish") has finally learned to enjoy what he finds. This transcendental fly fisher, it can be said, truly understands that the best place and the best time to go fishing are here and now. For those who are nevertheless curious about the proportions of the Eastern quarry, it should be reported that the East does contain many opportunities for larger fish. "A twenty-incher in every ditch" seems to be claimed as often as in the West. There are certainly big fish rivers in the East. The Delaware is one

example. Southern tailwaters like the Hiawasee and the Clinch often produce bragging size trout. Furthermore, for those fortunate to venture north of the border to the Atlantic salmon spawning rivers (only a handful of salmon now return to the streams of the northeastern United States), there is access to salmonid equal to any in the world. But as to trout, the fish we seek in the East are generally smaller than their relatives out West, especially in nutrient-poor southern Appalachian rivers. The exceptions to this rule are myriad. An average fish in the upper Little Wood of Idaho will be dwarfed by an average fish from the West Branch of the Ausable. An average fish from the Delaware will stand against most western trout except those from such hog farms as the San Juan and the Bighorn. But, a typical angler venturing out to home water in the drainages of the Appalachians, Catskills, and Adirondacks may have to find contentment with a smaller average catch and pleasure in being on the stream to fool the resident trout. And he seems, indeed, to find such satisfaction as readily as his western counterpart.

Besides the inevitable and tedious issue of the mass of the fish, our impressions (and Grant's photographs) reflect other

differences between East and West. With some notable exceptions, the settings in the East are more intimate, the backdrops more subtle in their beauty. To western eyes, the horizons appear limited; to Eastern eyes, these same horizons are close at hand, familiar and touchable. Regardless of these differences, the most striking idea that emerges from comparing our travels is that the essence of fly fishing knows no geographic differences. The water itself, its familiar pools, pockets, riffles and flow, and the unique and intimate beauty of eastern trout streams are enough to make a western angler feel at home in a heartbeat.

It was also reassuring to find that the folks we met on eastern streams were, just as in the West, genuine characters—gentle and generous in their dealings with fellow sportsmen and with their environment. Our travels in the streams of the East convinced us the experience of a local fisherman is every bit as rewarding as that of his western counterpart. Indeed, so was ours. The spiritual essence of fly fishing seems not to depend on the size of the fish, nor whether the fish live East or West, nor even, some would say, on the presence of a fish. For this writer at least, the sport continues to be the only activity that functions as a dependable escape valve from the slings and arrows of the real world. When an angler steps into a trout stream, he escapes into an entirely different world, a safe and comfortable hideaway. Our historic connection to the natural world, a connection that too often seems remote to many of us soon-to-be millennium crossers, is reestablished. A feeling resonates within us, a little unfamiliar but comfortable as Dad's easy chair. An ecstatic relaxation of body and mind dissolves time into organic renewal. Vaults open at the cellular level and, mysteriously, unknown and invisible components of the human body are sorted into more perfect order. We're fly fishing! We may not be ready to abandon our native West (it's

where we live), but we have no difficulty understanding why the eastern angler loves his fishing. We found great beauty in the rivers of the East and generous warmth and friendship in eastern anglers. All in all, there's a lot to like about the "first best place," the North American East.

FOUR YEARS AGO, in the preface to *Flywater,* I described my affection for the sport of fly fishing and related how my time on the trout stream may have contributed to a remarkable recovery from illness. Since then, I have heard from many cancer patients and their friends who have taken encouragement from that story. We have talked as fellow sufferers, veterans of foreign wars, of treatments, prognoses, and side effects, of good and bad doctors and medicines, and usually, before the conversation ends, of the therapeutic value of fly fishing. We resolve to "get out on the stream soon." During these intervening four years, I have continued to enjoy good health and I continue to believe that, for some, fly fishing can exercise the mind-body connection to promote a healing effect. Whether or not my experience has any general validity, fly fishing is assuredly a good way to spend a portion of our limited time on the *real* Planet Earth, in communion with one of her best features, our rivers, and finest creatures, the trout. What better metaphors exist for the healing process than the hydrologic cycle and the flow of a stream? My advice for those who may be struggling now with challenges I faced a few years ago is the same as it was then: Strive to be positive. Begin each day with thanks for another twenty-four-hour slice of time. And may you be wise and fortunate to spend some of those days standing in cool clear rivers.

TELLURIDE, COLORADO

DECEMBER 1997

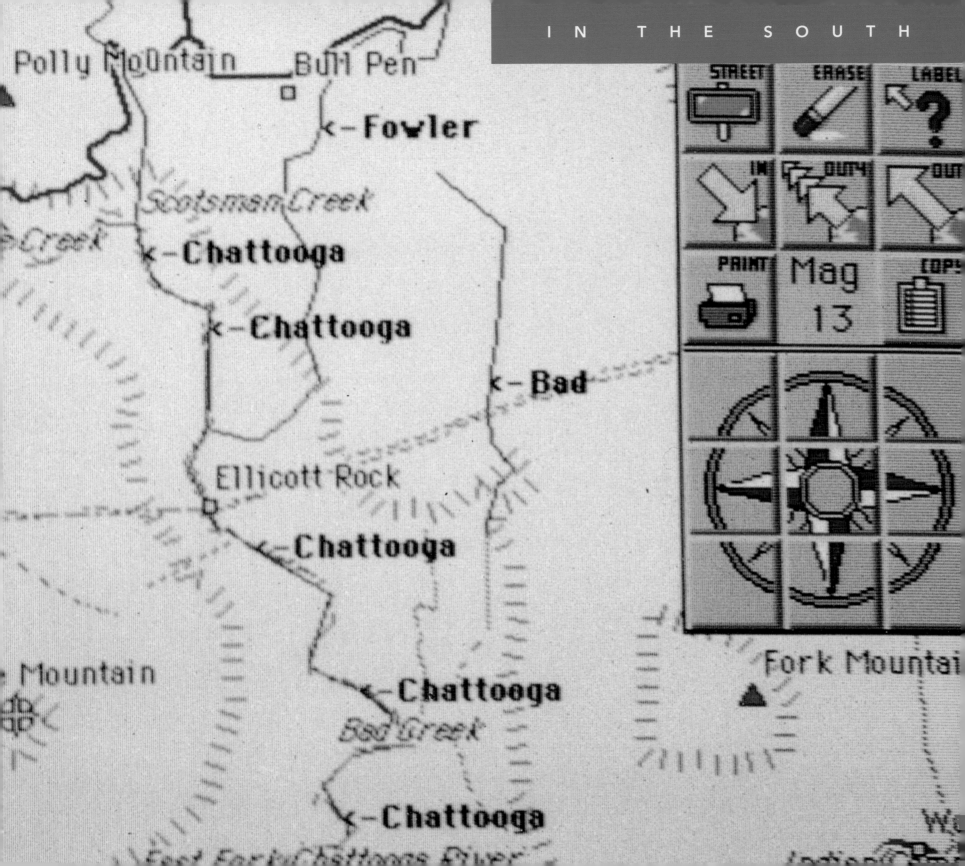

Henry

G R A N T   M c C L I N T O C K

ENRY tugs at his shirt—a blue Oxford button-down yuppie cast-off. "Fifty cents, Salvation Army. Know what these things cost new, brother?" He gazes at me for a moment with dusty gray puppy eyes, and I am forced to wonder if this is a real question.

Henry Williamson and I are cascading down the mountain in his enthusiastically trashed Toyota Tercel with 180K on the odometer. The car is ankle deep in garbage in the passenger compartment and in the back stacked half way to the ceiling—a court bouillon of trash and fishing gear. A couple of mice summer in Henry's car. If they happen to be home when he heads out, they go to the river with him.

It is 6:30 in the morning and "slap dark" as they say here in north Georgia. We are shooting down the mountain on which Henry built his family's home. Considering the 10 percent grade, the near ceaseless snaking of the road and the lack of light, thirty

miles per hour would be an adventure. Henry holds it at about fifty except on the rare straights where gravity and dependable Toyota engineering conspire to produce a sort of death wish free-fall speed.

The night before, Paula and I had ascended this very mountain. Our progress was quite different from my flight down with Henry the next morning. We were driving an almost new three-quarter-ton 454 Suburban pulling an insistently ponderous Airstream. Although we crept up the mountain at about fifteen mph, the drive was not without its own special terror. On this, my second day of pulling the beast (and first time in the mountains), the promise that the rather small steel ball attached to the back of my truck was sufficient to hold the behemoth on a 10 percent grade seemed as unlikely as calculus. Paula and I quietly and soberly awaited the expected, sickening sound—a low pitched, violent crack as the ball gave way, and we were offered a rearview

Chattooga River, Georgia

mirror vision of our new home separating like a rocket booster in NASA faux slow motion, accelerating and finally shooting back down the mountain at celestial speeds. The ball held, and after twenty minutes of strain, we crested the grade.

We were dressed out in the best Patagucci fashion. We have years of this stuff. Our ample stereo system belted out the new Van Morrison. Our three goldens slept blissfully unaware. The truck was full of fly rods, Nikons, groovy indigo back packs, an Apple laptop. The Airstream held various chutneys, an Italian espresso machine, an Alpine stereo, pointlessly expensive soap.

I had been given Henry's name by the best friend of a best friend. I was informed that he runs an Orvis fly fishing school in north Georgia not far from Highlands, North Carolina—goat cheese snarfing epicenter for the area. I was told that perhaps I could park by his house. I am envisioning a rather long driveway up to a modest but hip business—the trout pond to the left, the dog run full of frenetic pointers to the right. I picture a Gore-Tex laden Henry walking out to greet us with a warm smile glowing beneath his snap-brim Filson, a Nissan stainless coffee cup in hand. And so I phoned Henry and said I would like to meet him. Without missing a beat, Henry insisted that I come straight to his house and put my Airstream in his yard. Great. But what about this voice? Imagine the middle-aged love child of Gomer Pyle and Aunt Bea inviting you to drag your trailer by the house, and there you have Henry's accent. Now that's redneck. That's cracker.

We pulled into Henry's driveway just after dark. A slender figure of six feet, hunched against the cold, ambled down from the house to meet us, his hands pushed into his jeans pockets, thumbs out. "Well, ya made it," said Henry, and we shook on it. He touched the brim of his ball cap and began calling Paula "ma'am."

Henry had been busy preparing for our arrival. He had torn down a dog pen leaving a nice concrete pad, cut back the overgrowth of rhododendrons, and run electricity and water to the site. In short, he had created a miniature trailer park with "hard hook-up."

"Think this'll work?"

"If I can get the trailer in there."

The space Henry had in mind looked about right for an MG-B on blocks. Tight. And the pad tilted forward at a noticeable angle—excellent for hosing off dog crap, not so good for leveling a four-ton Airstream.

"Oh, we'll get her in all right."

"You think?"

Amazingly, with only an ordinary Oklahoma driver's license, I am actually allowed by law to back up an Airstream. They might as well let me do liver transplants. I am told this reversing is a simple task, but to me the angles are tricky and the whole process is overburdened with logic. Perhaps one day I will become proficient at this (although if there is a God, I will not be living in a trailer that long), but at the moment my approach to backing the behemoth is as follows: Put the truck in reverse and start backing up. If the trailer is not going where you want, turn the wheel the other way. This approach had worked very well for me in a WalMart parking lot just around midnight. In the less forgiving quarters of Henry's ex-dog pen, the weakness of my method quickly became apparent. After several fitful approaches, we arrived at a sensible way to proceed. Henry stood on one side of the trailer and Paula on the other. When one yelled, I turned the wheel. If that same person began screaming, I turned it the other way. Worked fine.

We finally got the Airstream on the pad and stepped inside to check it out. The trailer lurched forward and to the left making standing no sure thing. Henry peered around for a moment. I thought he was about to say, "This'll work," but instead it was, "I can fix this."

And so the leveling process began. As you might expect of someone who built his own house solo, Henry seemed to have an endless supply of odd-length boards. He had me back up a bit, pull up a bit, back up again. All the while, he was scurrying around placing and replacing boards under the tires. At this point, Henry's wife and two children joined in, and it seemed as if much of Rabun County was hard at work in order to assure me a nice level night's sleep. Henry's son, Hank, was sent off for a particular block of wood secreted under the house. The boy bounced off enthusiastically after answering his father's request, "Yessir." By the time Henry and his family had finished, the twenty-five-foot putt from the sofa at the front of the trailer to bathroom door at the rear rolled pool-table flat. This same putt had had a tough left to right break back in my driveway in Tulsa.

"COULD YA SWALLOW A BISCUIT?" Henry asks as we turn onto the relative flat of highway 441 and start north.

Ahead I see the enthusiastic reds and yellows of a McDonalds and, beyond the arches, the less commercial blue-gray hint of dawn. The McDonalds' sausage biscuit—staple breakfast of all-night alcoholics, befuddled wanderers and duck hunters—is tasty beyond belief.

I offer to pay. Henry shakes it off. When I try being a bit insistent, he looks over and, in the tone of the exasperated parent, says, "It ain't about money, brother."

We are headed north to fish some don't-even-ask private water. A certain stretch of a certain river is the domain of a private club which dates way, way back. The clubhouse is a simple but well proportioned cottage afloat on a manicured verdant patch which sweeps down to the river. The main room of the clubhouse holds an expanse of dining table at one end and an impressive river rock fireplace at the other. On the wall hang four or five slab trout which I assumed were imported from Alaska, New Zealand or the Bighorn. But wait. These fish are speaking to me—not in the coarse cloth of language but rather in some sort of trout telepathy. An electric blue bolt of awareness arcs through the ether. The biggest trout on the wall says, "Hey, wanker, don't you get it? We were all caught right here in the little river outside that window. Caught by important entrepreneurs and famous visiting anglers, neither of which you are, by the way." I suddenly realize that the trout speaks the truth, and I gaze out at this river respectfully.

Henry and I are to share a beat today. We arrive at our assigned stretch of river in Henry's wreck Toyota. Henry leaps from the car, and there begins a metamorphosis no less profound than caterpillar to butterfly. He leaves the car a redneck good ole boy in jeans and a fifty-cent shirt but enters the river a full blown

maddening frequency in the rhododendrons rather than the river. After five minutes, it becomes apparent that line control is not much of an issue in Henry's life. He has been fly fishing these waters for over a quarter of a century. His rod and line have attained a life of their own separate from piddling human will.

Henry's rig is familiar enough—the ubiquitous twin-nymph-with-indicator setup. Placing his weight between the two nymphs is the only hint of quirkiness. With the omnipresent cigarette hanging French auto mechanic style from the corner of his mouth, Henry chats amiably about this and that as he works upriver—all the while his rod flicking the fly first to the nearby slick, then in that little seam under the overhanging rhododendron, then a bit upstream just below the boulder. He appears a mildly interested observer attached at the right hand to some sort of

modern fly fisherman dripping with Simms, Orvis and Winston. The transformation is so startling that one is tempted to ask, "Henry, is that you?" But as he turns to me and says, " 'm on, brother, fish with me for a spell," the inner truth is revealed. I slip into the river behind Henry, a Nikon and 20mm lens dangling from my neck.

Contrary to custom, Henry uses a very long rod to fish the tight, overgrown southern Appalachian rivers. Most anglers opt for eight or less feet of fly rod. Henry uses a ten-foot Winston four weight. The extra length is useful in controlling the fly's drift (a major concern in this nervous pocket water), but unless you have extraordinary line control, a ten footer will put your fly with

automated harvester. When on occasion he sticks one in a tree (as all anglers on these rivers do from time to time), he eases over to liberate his fly with no interruption in the conversation nor reference to the mishap—just a slight sideward glance at the offending tree as if to aid in recalibrating the universe.

Wild trout in southern Appalachian freestones are, in a couple of words, generally small—or more to the point, small when compared to trout from other regions. Every river is purported to hold the twenty-inch exception, but, as a rule, small is not too harsh a word. A twelve-inch trout is a real prize in these freestones. It is a hardscrabble life for these fine fish. The rivers are basically nutrient poor, producing relatively few of the insects which are the staple food of growing trout. As if a marginal food supply weren't tough enough on the wild trout, at any moment their cozy little mountain home can be invaded by a truckload of hungry, ill-mannered hatchery fish. (There goes the neighborhood.) As meals can be hard to come by, wild trout grab them where they can. Never would you accuse these fish of being finicky eaters. Unlike their Western brethren at, say, Silver Creek, where the quantity of food makes a Viking feast look like nouvelle cuisine, these southern trout are grateful for every scrap that comes their way. The Silver Creek aristocrats grow fat and wise at their leisure. No need for those big boys to dart out from behind a rock into hard-on current for a fleeting shot at a #20 nymph. No, they simply pick from the fray a target, rise deliberately, take a good look and (if it's not some funky tied fly) have a bite. While the challenging environment may slow the growth of southern Appalachian wild trout, it also culls the weaklings, the slightly slow, the less aggressive. These fish stay in fighting fiddle or they don't stay at all. They understand a tussle, as they willingly demonstrate when hooked.

Thirty minutes pass, and Henry has picked up two fish of twelve inches or so. "You'll never hear me complain, but this is slow for this place." How right he was. Later that day I saw Henry slam five trout, all over fourteen inches, out of one run. During one period the water went slightly roily from up-stream bridge work. The fish turned on, perhaps sensing security in the milkiness, and I was witness to the landing of a stunning twenty-inch-plus rainbow.

In the angler's world, the bigger the fish the better—but not always. An ten-inch wild brown from the upper Chattooga in Georgia is fundamentally (one is tempted to say morally) superior to the twenty-two-inch pellet-eating pig slopped into some tailwa-ter in Oklahoma (my beloved home state) by Fish & Game and the Bank of Commerce to spice up the big Labor Day weekend. Land the latter and you get your picture in the paper plus a coin bank in the shape of a sailfish. Catch the little wild brown on a light fly rod with a fine tippet and you pull into one of the many pleasant stations along the line where man and fish get together. At this particular stop the trout may be light but the ritual has weight.

I watch Henry release another large, ruby streaked rainbow. Why does this stretch of club water hold such an array of monster trout? Naturally (or perhaps unnaturally), the membership has decided to rectify Mother Nature's oversight and supply their fish with an ample serving of trout chow. It would be hard to imagine a piece of water more perfectly managed for growing big trout in a natural environment. I had thought the trout would be found in odd lies dictated by the feeding stations, but this was not the case. The fish were caught where trout should be caught and seemed perfectly capable of finding food in the stream. But between bug meals they happily gobble up the Purina and get fat. As Henry observed, "It's artificial but a lot of fun."

I ARRIVE AT THE WELDING SHOP with a little styrofoam cup, an offering, held before me. Encircling the top of the cup are a dozen of Henry's beautifully tied flies. Henry has set out to fix the malfunctioning latch on our Airstream. He needs a bit of emergency welding done and Frank, also a fly fisherman, is the man. Henry is a true southerner and, it follows, a great believer in the power of gifts. He had arrived at the private club laden with jellies and jams, a shadow box of flies and a jar of cheap hotdogs. When I showed up with two gift books for the club under my arm, Henry commented, "You're gonna do fine in the South."

Henry had given me the fly-ringed cup as a sop for Frank—"to grease the wheel." Frank-the-welder, it seems, is a long term fly fisher. He is short and solid—like a pit bull, and with the same underlying promise of violence. He wipes his hands with a greasy red cloth, takes the cup and gives the flies a perfunctory glance. He sets the rig on one of the many metal tables in his shop. His only comment: "Henry owes me those."

I show him the small broken part. He holds it still, close to his face and moves his head around to assess the damage. "That'll want a TIG."

Five minutes later I am holding the repaired part and handing Frank a five-dollar bill. Cheap, I think.

The successful completion of the TIG operation has noticeably lightened Frank's spirits, or perhaps the heavy drug of a fly-ringed styrofoam cup has finally kicked in. At any rate, I detect what could be construed as a smile.

"How's Henry?" he begins.

"Good."

"You staying up there?"

"Yeah."

"Tell him to call me."

"Sure. You been fishing?"

"Went Saturday."

"Do any good?"

"Everybody got a limit."

In southern Appalachia the fly fishing habit and the eating habit are not generally seen as incompatible.

PAULA AND I ARE PACKING for a fishing and photo trip up the Chattooga, one of north Georgia's finest trout streams. To look at us you might think we were headed into the Gobi wilderness for a month. The biggest backpack I own is loaded down with fishing gear, camera gear, food, drink, snacks for the dogs, snacks for the humans, cosmetics, various creams for various health concerns, rain gear (it's seventy degrees and sunny) and ample miscellany.

Among other distinctions, the Chattooga was selected as the location for the filming of *Deliverance*. I query Henry as to the true nature of the natives.

"Ah," said Henry. "You won't likely see anything but other yuppies up there. Although. . . last month there was two couples from Atlanta camped there with a big ole Labrador retriever. They had set up a real nice camp—North Face tents, little green folding chairs. They were stirring dinner and having some wine when they heard a terrible commotion up on the mountain. They looked up there and here come a 300-pound mountain man with a beard to his belly. He stormed into their camp, grabbed up the first man, head-butted him unconscious and tossed him in the river. He kicked the second man in the groin and threw him in the river right behind the first one. He headed towards one of the women to do Lord knows what when he saw that big Labrador. He yanked up the dog, cut off a ham and ate it raw. He wiped off his mouth, turned to the women and said, 'I'm sure sorry. I was raised better 'n this. I know it's rude to eat and run, but I gotta go. There a really bad man coming behind me.'"

We began our hike upriver at Burrell's Ford, about four and a half miles below the North Carolina border. Downriver from Burrell's Ford the Chattooga is heavily stocked (by helicopter). Most of the stocked fish are rainbows, but you will stumble onto the odd brown and somewhat odder brookie. Upstream from Burrell's Ford there is no stocking. This section is known for its abundance of wild brown trout, reason enough to head upstream.

Avery Creek, North Carolina

About 190 years ago, a fellow named Andrew Ellicott was sent out to determine the borders of Georgia, North Carolina and South Carolina. Having located the spot on the Chattooga where the three states meet, he carved the date, 1813, into a boulder by the river—Ellicott Rock. This would be a useful landmark to modern day anglers indicating where the Georgia fishing license runs out of gas and the North Carolina license comes into play. Unfortunately the rock is all but unfindable. The Forest Service has provided a sign, but it is vague at best and, at worst, absent—removed perhaps as a playful prank by some kinder, gentler mountain man of the '90s.

Paula strings up the little Orvis Brook Trout rod with an old Pfleuger reel. My once petite and delicate Winston nine-foot four weight feels like a steelhead stick after a few weeks on these tight rivers. There are no bugs, no fish rising, but Paula ties on an elk hair caddis and wades out into the Chattooga.

She begins in the tail-out of a long pool. The water is off color from a day of hard rain. The fish are reluctant, but she is into it now, fanning casts across the water, mending the line, trying for the perfect drift. The game is on.

I drop in behind a Nikon. It is like climbing into a warm bed with a good book on a chilly evening. I am completely comfortable with the near future. I am interested without being anxious, alert but relaxed. This optically-adjusted world is my domain and provides a rare isle of confidence in the ocean of doubt. Here the decisions are mine, and I make them quickly but with certainty and an underlying sense of purpose and passion.

Paula is finally rewarded with a fish—a small one and a swim-up rainbow, not the brown trout we are here to visit. She takes a break. Standing on a slightly submerged rock she rests the back of her left hand against her cocked hip and, while gazing downriver, applies Chapstick with the right hand. I touch the shutter button.

THE NEXT MORNING I return to Henry's house to find a Mercedes, a Range Rover and a motorcycle parked in the driveway. The Orvis fly fishing school is open for business.

Henry has his band of five students lined up along the trout pond. He has begun with the roll cast—technique *de rigueur* in this part of the country, where a full blown overhead cast is as rare as foot-long native brookies. The rods rise and slap down in the sudden, jerky movements of windup toys. The lines bundle up just beyond the rod tips.

Henry is all enthusiasm and energy. He moves from one student to the next. It is very much a hands-on lesson. He guides these new arms through the proper movement, and slowly things begin to improve. "See, I told you you'd get it. It's really not hard."

Henry's energetic nature comes courtesy of genetics and the Lipton Tea Company. "Sweet Tea" sounds simple enough. It is what it says it is, but a bit more. Here is Henry's recipe. To a quart of water add four tea bags and three *cups* of sugar. Boil vigorously for ten minutes. Dilute to taste. Henry dilutes his to make a gallon. This is almost embarrassingly weak by the accepted southern-church-social caffeine standard, but what Henry misses through dilution he makes up for in quantity. In the morning Henry comes out of the blocks with a few cups of coffee like any good American. Once sentient, he moves to the more potent sweet tea, and he rides this caffeine pony with grim junkie determination all day long. He is never far from his jug. In Henry's opinion, if you order sweet tea in a restaurant and the waitress gives you a funny look, you should get up and go. You have left the civilized world. For us, one of the charms of travel is the opportunity to acquire new addictions. Paula now regularly boils up sweet tea like a Georgia grit.

Henry is forty-two, and he claims that he is beginning to slow down just a bit. Hard to see. He fishes almost every day after his work—jobs which range from the genteel art of teaching Atlantans to fly fish to trenching out sewer lines or re-roofing the cottages of "summer people." For Henry, work is a regrettably necessary interruption in the twenty-four-hour fishing day. In distant halcyon hippie days, such interruptions were kept to the near monastic level of bare necessity. Odd jobs (apiarist for hire, Forest Service drone) served all the needs of youth. But with a wife and two children, the role of inveterate fishhead began to look more irresponsible than romantic, so Henry cut back a bit. But not too much. He still puts in a hundred days a year fly fishing. I once asked Joyce, Henry's preternaturally good-natured wife, if his compulsive fishing caused the family any stress. I could see at once the question struck her as odd. "Well, you see," she finally answered, "We like him that way."

HENRY'S IMMEDIATE FAMILY and one set of grandparents have headed for Myrtle Beach. He is to join them tomorrow. Tonight he is dining with us in the Airstream. We cook up a stir fry, break out the decent wine and cigars. We set up the vise and Henry shows me a few tricks. I have started tying orange caddis and dark-winged orange duns. These imitate no creature in God's vision of north Georgia, but I have come to believe in the color orange for these Georgia trout. This belief is based on almost nothing. The first day I caught a couple of fish on an orange fly Henry had tied—enough to transmogrify an anemic hope into a vibrant doctrine which will, no doubt, last for the rest of my life. I picture myself, an eighty-five-year-old geezer warming his hands by the fireplace with fellow anglers at the new Orvis lodge in recently annexed Uganda. The subject of Appalachian trout comes up. I let the young men chatter until, removing my cigar from the tracheotomy incision, I croak out one word, "Orange." I replace the cigar. The young sprats fall silent and nod deferentially.

We talk about the fish we've caught and seen caught back through the years. The funny ones are the best, but the big ones aren't bad either.

Henry notices the proud little parade of medication lined up behind my bed. Pravachol, Enduron, etc. Each brown plastic pillar attesting to one more thing not working quite right inside.

I ask Henry if he has to take any drugs.

"No, not really. I'll take a Valium if I have to fly, and every now and then I take Prozac,"—pronouncing Prozac as if it had one syllable per letter. He sees that I am surprised, rather shocked to find him in need of the ubiquitous American restorative of recent years. He looks up sheepishly. "I get a little depressed some time," he says.

Don't we all, brother. Don't we all.

HENRY LOADS UP THE CAR for the sojourn to Myrtle Beach. Out come waders, rods, fishing vests—in go beach towels, an Igloo, a bag of kites. Henry is a builder of exquisite, delicate kites. He took us to a mountain top one windy evening where we watched one of his creations dart about the fading Georgian sky like a martin on mosquitoes.

He throws in a few books. I have slowly learned over the course of our visit that this cracker is far better read than I.

One of the neighbors arrives with a child in tow. Henry is taking this young'un along to the beach. The boy shows Henry the twenty-dollar bill he has been given for the trip. "I'll have that twenty 'fore we get out Georgia," says Henry. The boy looks worried. Henry ruffles the kid's hair, "Naw, you keep that. I'll get the gas this time."

Henry has taken to calling me The Bohemian with a violent accent on the first syllable. It amuses him, as do my quite un-bohemian concerns that our life is badly misdirected and will shortly develop into full-blown nightmare. He admonishes me, "You gotta work on that *Bo*hemian attitude. You're a lucky fella. I had your job, I'd never get out of the river and wouldn't worry about it either."

He jumps into the driver's seat, sticks his hand through the window. We shake. "Stay in touch." The car disappears down his gravel driveway, and Paula and I are left standing in a little swirl of north Georgia dust.

YESTERDAY I TURNED FIFTY. We always drink a bottle or two of Veuve Cliquot on such momentous occasions and spend a lot of time fussing over the food. We decided on rainbow trout meunière for the birthday dinner. Henry had directed us to catch some fish from the trout pond. "You'll want three apiece," he said, but two were plenty.

Lynn Camp Prong, Tennessee

Laurel Fork, Virginia

Crawford Creek, North Carolina

The rhododendron-lined
trout streams of southern
Appalachia are among the
country's loveliest. However,
the rhododendron and other
riparian flora exact a price
for all this beauty,
voraciously swallowing up
any misdirected back-cast.
On many streams, the roll
cast is the preferred method
of delivering fly to water.

Abrams Creek, Tennessee

Panthertown Creek, North Carolina

Bath County, Virginia

Panthertown Creek, North Carolina

Panthertown and Greenland require a bit of hiking to reach, but the reward is ample—rising native trout swimming in pristine mountain streams. These two North Carolina creeks are highland Appalachian fly fishing at its purest.

Overflow Creek, Georgia

Laurel Fork, Virginia

The Jackson River of Virginia offers a variety of water to suit your mood. Depending on where you step into the river, you will fish an excellent tailwater, a classic freestone, or a languid meadow stream. To this wealth of choice add a healthy population of fish fed by a swarm of insect life, and you have one of the South's most enjoyable trout streams.

South Holston River, Tennessee

There is no substitute for local knowledge. On the South Holston, a tailrace with frequent changes in water level, a friend who knows where the fish will lie when the river falls is a valuable companion.

Crawford Creek, North Carolina

South Holsten River, Tennessee

The native trout of
Southern Appalachia
inhabit their high
mountain streams
with aboriginal
dignity. These
brookies are
stunningly beautiful,
scrappy and willing.
Plus the average one
will fit conveniently
in the palm of your
hand.

Yellowstone Prong, North Carolina

Middle Prong Little River, Tennessee

The rivers and streams of southern Appalachia are rife with waterfalls, among the loveliest being the string of cataracts which sends Cascades Creek tumbling away from the town of Warm Springs, Virginia.

Dry Run, Virginia

54

Looking Glass Falls, North Carolina

Dry Run, Virginia

Jackson River, Virginia

Beaverkill River, New York

IF YOU'RE WORRIED that legions of Laphroaig-swilling, Cohiba-puffing, money-shoveling Philistines are gumming up the works on your favorite stream in the cradle of American fly fishing civilization—I have in mind here the Catskills, but you could pick any number of northeastern trout rivers—then take heart. Things didn't look so swell 121 years ago either, as long-dead voices make clear in Ed Van Put's fine book *The Beaverkill.*

"The number of both City and Country who affect to be 'trout fishers' is largely increased," the Rev. Dr. E.W. Bently wrote in the front page of the *Ellenville Journal* on July 20, 1877. "It is said to be a rule in New York business circles that all applicants for positions of any kind, from that of bar tender up through all grades of clerkships to a silent partnership, must be provided with a trout pole, fly-book and fish basket. No man or boy can 'come

the gorilla' in the stock exchange who doesn't own or can't borrow a German silver mounted fly pole . . . The last time I was on the Beaverkill I encountered, rod in hand and creel on his back, a tailor's apprentice, fresh from Gotham, in a brand new suit of silver-grey corduroys! And in the country, the highway from boyhood to manhood leads through a trout stream as certainly as through a cigar box. Hence the poor trout have next to no chance at all."

Yet somehow the trout have survived, be it in the Willowemoc, the Beaverkill, the Delaware or any of a score of eastern streams where for a couple of centuries bandy-legged Yankees have been taking their ease by tossing wads of fur and feathers at speckled ichthyoids. Not that we haven't done our best to wipe out the various salmos that either God placed in the Catskills or that we imported after denuding the aboriginal stock.

Joan Wulff, 1952 National Casting Tournament

First the train, then the automobile, brought hordes of anglers who hauled wagonloads of trout from the Beaverkill and other streams with heedless abandon. Then our forefathers hacked down the timber that covered the hills above the rivers. Next, they brought in the tanneries that pumped noxious effluvium into these clear mountain streams. Somewhere along the line, we unleashed the stocked fish that have simultaneously denigrated indigenous brook trout while, over the decades, creating a new brown trout fishery that isn't half bad. Finally, not long ago, the state rammed a four-lane highway, Route 17, through the fishy heart of the Catskills, annually bringing in hundreds of thousands of vehicles that squash and splat millions of mayflies, not to mention providing anglers with the distinctly depressing experience of listening to the whoosh of cars and the rumble of trucks while standing waist-deep in a stream.

So I ask you: Next to these onslaughts, where's the harm in a pretty little movie like *A River Runs Through It*? So what if Robert Redford unleashed on America's streams a small army of neoprene-swaddled neophytes with spastic casting styles and more airs than a down-on-his-luck French count? This, too, shall pass. Fortunately, the desire to ride the crest of the latest trend is not a motivation that will sustain a man or a woman on a trout stream, and so the faddists inevitably fall away. What's left are the people who love to fish.

ON A JANUARY AFTERNOON, with low, lead-gray clouds threatening snow, I drove from my home just outside New York City to the epicenter of the historic Catskills fishery, the Beaverkill and Willowemoc rivers. Though it had been a dismally warm and rainy winter and fishing was possible on the still-unfrozen streams, I did not drive towards Livingston Manor with a fly rod in my trunk. I went instead with a notepad, for I wanted to talk with two people who knew East Coast fly fishing about as well as anyone, anglers who could take the long view of the sport. One was Ed Van Put, who knows more about the history of Catskills fly fishing than anyone alive. The other was Joan Wulff, America's best-known woman fly fisher, even before she married Lee Wulff, the man whose name always seems to be preceded by the adjective "legendary." Joan Wulff has been making a living in fly fishing for half a century, and would, I figured, have something to say about the burgeoning popularity of the sport and its attendant commercialization.

I found Joan Wulff at the large, well-groomed compound that she and her late husband established at Lew Beach on the upper Beaverkill twenty years ago. The family spread is situated in a scenic valley, with the river on one side and steep, thickly forested hills on the other. Nestled under the low mountains is the main house, a handsome, recently-built structure covered in white aluminum siding. It is surrounded by a host of outbuildings, some of which are used for the Wulff School of Fly Fishing. Lower down is the wide, hay-colored meadow that Lee Wulff—who died in 1991 at the age of eighty-six—used as a landing strip for his Piper Super Cub. Beyond the meadow is a country road, and just past that is the Beaverkill, which in a normal January would have been covered with ice, but on this day was flowing green and clear.

At seventy-one Joan Wulff is still a striking woman, with short, curly, gray hair, hazel eyes, and a slender physique. Wearing a fushcia sweater and gray pants, she ushered me into her cathedral-ceilinged living room. The walls are adorned with watercolors depicting some of Canada's greatest salmon rivers and a caribou head is centered above the fireplace. The house is not a shrine to Lee Wulff, the century's best-known American fly fisherman, but his presence is palpable: in his old fly-tying nook near the kitchen, in the sculptures and paintings that reflect his lifelong devotion to the Atlantic salmon, in the gear and tackle that are still in the house, and in the hundreds of cannisters of film stored on shelves in the basement, the remnants of the scores of outdoor programs he did for television.

Though she was at times overshadowed by this man with towering accomplishments and an ego to match, Joan Wulff has had her own remarkable, half-century career in fly fishing. Since winning her first casting championship at twelve, she has been caught up in the changes that have swept the sport, changes that have turned a modest, often blue-collar pastime into a chi-chi activity that has spawned an absurd quantity of books, analysis, chatter, bullshit and not a few egomaniacs who seem to think that the pursuit of angling nirvana is on a par with the effort to map the human genome.

Joan Wulff came to fly fishing the old fashioned way—she learned it, on her own, slowly and steadily, driven by an inexplicable attraction to casting and rivers and fish. Her father, Jimmy Salvato, owned an outdoor store in Paterson, New Jersey, and Joan grew up casting and fishing with a crew of down-home craftsmen who worked in wood and metal.

Few women were fly fishing at mid-century, and soon Joan Salvato found herself winning casting championship after casting championship, sometimes even beating the men. In her twenties, she combined her love of dancing and fly fishing, and earned a few bucks at angling shows by donning hip boots and short shorts to give casting demonstrations. Before long, she graduated to a show in which she put on casting demonstrations—often with fly rods in both hands—while wearing a strapless, ankle-length white gown, high-heeled sandals, and rhinestones in her hair. Performing to the tune "Up A Lazy River" and working with emcee Monte Blue, an aging silent screen star, Joan Salvato wowed audiences by painting graceful pictures in the air with her fly lines.

Eventually she went to work for the Ashaway Line & Twine Company, promoted fishing tackle for the Garcia Corporation, married Lee Wulff, opened a fly fishing school, and created Royal Wulff Products, a small outfit that sells fly lines, videos, and some fishing gear. She seems as surprised as anyone that she has made a living doing what she loves.

"I never dreamed that I would end up with so rich a life," said Mrs. Wulff, sitting in her living room as an employee struggled with a recalcitrant computer in a back room. "I never figured that it was a career that would go anywhere. I just did it because I loved it."

In her own small way, Joan Wulff has been responsible for popularizing the sport and bringing hordes of new anglers to the nation's streams. Having played a part in boosting fly fishing in the nation's consciousness to the level of golf or tennis, Mrs. Wulff is left with decidedly mixed emotions.

"Now they're too many fishermen. The rivers are pounded so much. You just can't go to the river and fish in a place where you used to be alone. Now you'll find other fishermen there. Those who manage the resource may have to start restricting how many people can be in an area at a given time.

"But I happen to love fly fishing and think everyone ought to experience it. It takes you to such beautiful places. I can't imagine that people who do not experience the outdoors can live a full life. And we need new anglers to protect the resource. If I weren't bringing new people to the sport, someone else would be, so it is extremely important to stress the value of the resource."

After nearly six decades in the business, Joan Wulff is heartened that at last large numbers of women are entering the sport. Perhaps more than anyone else, she can claim credit for changing the overwhelmingly masculine face of fly fishing, acting as a mentor to numerous women fishermen, guides and outfitters who have, in turn, introduced scores of other women to the sport.

"I think women are the single biggest growth area," said Mrs. Wulff. "It's great. I've been waiting all my life for this. I've always known how wonderful fly fishing was and now a lot of women know it too. I now have women friends who love fishing as much as I do."

Joan Wulff is in a good position to observe one of the paradoxes of today's angling world. With more people fly fishing and the number of lodges, guides, and outfitted trips expanding exponentially, the frontiers of fishing are shrinking. As fishing opportunities have become accessible to anyone with a Visa Gold, they have become tame. And Joan Wulff knows wild. Her husband used to hop in his airplane and fly over the wilderness of Newfoundland and Labrador, landing when the spirit moved him, fishing for salmon in rivers where few, if any, men had fished before. Joan Wulff also experienced first tracks fishing from Canada to the Caribbean.

She accepts with equanimity that the frontiers in angling are disappearing. This is the century, after all, when travel has given way to tourism. And she is too gracious to pass judgment on some of the well-heeled anglers who seem to feel they can buy their way into fly fishing as they would acquire a company. Still, she is plainly uneasy that, to some, fly fishing has become a money-scented pastime, with end-of-the-millennium pashas busy notching trophy vacation in their belts—Ponoi, Patagonia, Pond's.

"Now, if people have the money and the time they can buy

the experience," said Mrs. Wulff. "They buy the guides, the ranches. Anyone who has the desire and the money can taste all this—the trout fishing, bone-fishing, any top-notch angling. That's the biggest difference from my day. Then you had to really put in the time. It will be interesting to see if the newcomers who expect instant gratification ever become real fishermen."

But to hell with the folks with the big money and the bad manners. If they pay for it, and don't really get it, then the joke's on them. Joan Wulff is still mesmerized by fly fishing because she's spent a lifetime trying to figure it out, and still hasn't succeeded.

"I personally like to fish public water. It's not as sure. I don't want sureness in my fishing. If I catch three fish on one fly, I change flies. If it was always easy, I'd go to another sport. The challenge, the unknown, the mystery—all of that keeps me coming back."

These days, when she has the time—which is not nearly as often as she would like—Joan Wulff wanders over to the Beaverkill, about a mile upstream from her house, and fishes one of her favorite pools. Holding a mix of wild and stocked trout, the pool is long and deep, the current swift at the top and slow-moving in the tail-out. "I know the fish there. They are friends but they're not always easy to catch," she said. "It's just a lovely pool."

She has fished nearly everywhere, but Joan Wulff is still drawn to the Beaverkill because of its history, muted beauty, and the intimacy of a stream that winds through wooded hills. She and her husband decided to settle down on the upper reaches of the Beaverkill because of all these things, and because—back in the late '70s—the Beaverkill had a four-mile "no kill" zone, which was uncommon at the time. Lee Wulff had been practicing catch-and-release for decades. "He'd like to be remembered more than anything else as the father of catch-and-release," said Mrs. Wulff.

"He loved fishing wherever he was. He wanted to fish as much as he could, and wherever he could, and I guess I've become that way, too. That's where I've wanted to be—wherever the trout were."

In 1991, at age eighty-six, Lee Wulff suffered a massive heart attack while piloting his Piper Super Cub near his home. He crashed with an FAA instructor who was recertifying Wulff's license, and was killed. Just a month earlier, Lee Wulff had spent more than three hours landing a sailfish off Costa Rica. Joan Wulff scattered his ashes on the Beaverkill, and wants hers cast into the river, as well.

"I tell people I am an ordinary woman who has had an extraordinary life through the magic of fly fishing," Mrs. Wulff told me as I prepared to leave. "And it really is magic—the idea of being able to throw a little bunch of feathers into a river and to be connected to a wild creature, and really feel its life force. And you do feel it. It's like electricity, only much softer and nicer."

ABOUT FIFTEEN MILES from the Wulff spread is the more modest hacienda of Ed Van Put and his wife, Judy O'Brien. Theirs is a brown-and-white shingle home surrounded by a grove of pine trees and plunked down hard by the road. But Ed Van Put's place has one decided

Ed Van Put.
Photo by Alan Fried

advantage. From it, he can almost spit into Willowemoc Creek, which is a good thing, since Van Put—who acquires public trout water for the New York State Department of Environmental Conservation—is a fishing fool. Except in winter, Van Put finds time to fish nearly every day, sometimes in the smaller, more subtle waters of the Beaverkill, Willowemoc or Esopus, but often in the Delaware River.

"I can firmly say that the Delaware River is the best trout stream east of the Mississippi," said Van Put.

Delving into natural history can sometimes be a depressing exercise, particularly if you're given to thinking, as I often am, that you've arrived on the scene about a century too late and that much of our fair land has been irrevocably befouled. But reading Van Put's book, *The Beaverkill,* and spending a few hours with him talking, drinking coffee, and wolfing down hot cinnamon buns was a heartening experience. How odd to contemplate this fact: That the town of Rockland—which includes fishing Meccas Roscoe and Livingston Manor and is only two hours' drive from the Empire State Building—has just 382 more residents now than it did in 1905. Or that the logging operations, lumber mills and tanneries that once polluted Catskill streams are virtually all gone, leaving the watershed far less polluted today than it has been in decades. Or that 45 percent of the woodlands in the region are now part of the state-created Catskill Forest Preserve and are protected from logging and development.

As I drove to see Van Put, I did not anticipate that he would casually announce, "I think the fishing's as good as it's ever been. Some old timers would disagree. But I know public streams here where I can still catch 100 fish in six hours."

Of course, he's not referring to the days before the white man, but all the same this is not what you'd expect to hear about the most storied fishery in the East, one that is visited annually by tens of thousands of angling refugees from the megalopolis.

As a reading of *The Beaverkill* makes clear, while a certain segment of the populace has done its best to screw up the Catskills fishery over the past two centuries, a dedicated band of anglers and conservationists—people like Van Put and Wulff—has rallied to its defense. Throughout the history of the Beaverkill and nearby streams, the same issues have played over and over like a refrain— overfishing, pollution, development, public water versus private water. Oddly enough, in many areas the good guys have won.

After the opening of the Erie Railroad in 1848, believers in the eternal bounty of the United States who rode the new train into the Catskills from New York City slaughtered fish by the ton. In 1855, the *Kingston Journal* reported "parties of gentlemen" hauling as many as 1,800 brook trout out of the Beaverkill in a few days' time. Seven years later Robert Barnwell Roosevelt wrote that "the country was literally overrun, and Bashe's Kill, Pine Kill, the Sandberg, the Mon Gap and Callicoon, and even the Beaverkill, which we thought were inexhaustible, were fished out. For many years, trout had almost ceased from out of these waters, but the horrible public, having their attention drawn to the Adirondacks, gave it a little rest."

Twenty years later, things looked even worse, as dandies from New York and other East Coast cities competed with western hunters to see which they could extirpate first—the brook trout, or the buffalo.

"*Salmo Fontinalis* is becoming small by degrees, and deplorably scarce," wrote George W. Sears, under the pseudonym Nessmuk, in *The American Angler* of 1881. "It is the constant, indefatigable working of the streams by skilled anglers, who turn out in brigades. . . . Anglers increase as trout diminish; and such

streams are infested by anglers from April to August, to an almost incredible extent, nearly all of whom basket anything more than four inches long. . . . The trout are playing out."

Somehow, in the Catskills, sportsmen managed to pull back from the brink, in part because they had decimated so many fish that angling became scarcely worth the effort. But other factors conspired to save the trout. Though some locals squawked, groups of fishermen, many from New York City, began to form private clubs along the Beaverkill, at last instituting some control over creel limits. In 1876, the first brook trout stocking took place on the Beaverkill. Seven years later, the U.S. Commission of Fisheries introduced the brown trout from Europe. *Salmo fario,* a creature that would adapt superbly to Catskill rivers, eventually moved in large numbers into the lower Beaverkill, whose waters were too warm to sustain brook trout. As the century drew to a close, tanning and logging operations slowed down or closed, giving brook and brown trout a little more breathing room.

Then a new wave of anglers flooded the area in the early part of the century as the first automobiles made their way from New York City to the Catskills. Many locals were appalled. "The residents of the sections where fishing is most popular are becoming enraged over the automobile parties who come on Sundays and spend the day fishing, taking fine strings back with them," the *Sullivan County Review* reported on May 6, 1915.

Still, with state officials at last imposing creel limits and with brown trout thriving, the fishing continued to improve. Enormous browns were showing up in the Beaverkill. In July 1926, Fred Shaver of Turnwood, New York, landed a brown trout that was twenty-eight inches long and weighed ten pounds.

By the 1960s, there were plenty of fish in the Beaverkill and nearby streams, but biologists were dismayed to find that more

than 90 percent of the trout caught by anglers were stocked fish. In 1964, the state introduced its first no-kill area, restricting a two-mile section of the lower Beaverkill to catch-and-release angling. Today, seven miles of catch-and-release areas exist on the Beaverkill, and more than a dozen more on the Willowemoc and the Delaware.

Sitting in Van Put's kitchen, with traces of snow drifting through the evergreens, I inquired whether the classic Beaverkill/Willowemoc fishery had been overrun in recent years by marauding yuppies. I was surprised by his answer.

"Honestly I think there were more fishermen here in the 1970s than there are now," said Van Put, an affable sixty-one-year-old with a full head of brown, silver-flecked hair and a pair of bushy commas for eyebrows. "But the fishermen are more spread out now and they're much better informed. I could always find a secret spot to fish on the Beaverkill or Willowemoc where there were no people. Now you can't do that."

There's been another big change—a sizable shift of anglers from the Beaverkill and Willowemoc to the Delaware, where many fish fanatics have lost their heads over the big, wild and often-elusive rainbow trout that inhabit the river. Van Put has succumbed to this temptation as well, and he fishes there frequently. Anglers have gravitated to the Delaware in part because a series of droughts in the 1990s and a devastating flood in 1996 have taken a toll on the Beaverkill watershed. The natural calamities were compounded by state and local officials who bulldozed into oblivion prime spawning habitat in an effort to clear debris-clogged creeks and streams. The Theodore Gordon Flyfishers organization is sufficiently concerned about the Beaverkill/Willowemoc fishery that it has launched a campaign to reduce reliance on stocking and make watershed improvements that will boost populations of wild trout.

This decade has, indeed, been a tough one on the "Beamoc" watershed, but Van Put, who moved to the area in 1964, is confident it will rebound. And despite the appeal of the Delaware's broad waters and muscular trout, Van Put often finds himself on the Beaverkill, Willowemoc and classic brook trout streams that have defined the Catskills. Part of the appeal of the Beaverkill watershed is its history. Van Put frequently finds himself fishing in spots where the likes of Theodore Gordon or A.J. McClane once pursued trout. The more Van Put learned about the Beaverkill, the more he realized how much it had stayed the same. For decades now, twenty-five of its forty-three miles—the upper portion—have been in private hands. No new private clubs have appeared on the Beaverkill in over a century; the last to be formed was the Brooklyn Fly Fishers, established in 1895.

Few people know the area as well as Van Put, enabling him to repair to remote streams where the fishing remains as it was a century or two ago. He knows a tributary of the Willowemoc that meanders through a glen of grassy hummocks where in early July, without a soul in sight, he can catch nine-inch wild brook trout until he's scratched that particular itch.

"Sometimes I'm just out there to satisfy this urge to catch a lot of fish," said Van Put. "I like the fact it's so primitive, and I like the solitude. I like fishing the small streams, not just because of the aesthetics, but also to simply see what's there. And practically every stream in the Catskills has a waterfall, and the plunge pools below them are special."

A few years ago, wandering deep into the woods along another small stream, he came upon a small beaver bond. Tying on a wet fly, he cast into the pool and began catching one twelve-inch, wild brook trout after another. He stood there for hours, catching and releasing dozens of fish.

"As much as I fish, it was still awesome," Van Put recalled. "It was so good, there was so much activity, and the fish were of such quality that it was almost like it should have been against the law."

Van Put is now at work on a history of the entire Catskills fishery, a project that he fervently hopes will consume less time than the thirteen years it took him to produce *The Beaverkill.* Before leaving, I asked him what would become of this legendary fishery in thirty years.

"I don't know," he said. "I've lived here more than thirty years and for all practical purposes nothing has changed. The resiliency of the nature here is incredible. We've seen years of environmental disturbances, most recently the bulldozing of streams. Things have happened to streams here that if they happened to streams closer to the city they would never recover. It's a wonder of nature, how things can be abused and bounce back."

I said goodbye to Van Put and his wife and drove along the Willowemoc before turning on a road that paralleled the Beaverkill. A steady wind carried a fine snow that still had not stuck to the ground. Scarcely a car was on the road. The sky and the forest merged into monochromatic gray. I stopped at a long, shallow run, the clear, dark water moving briskly over the stones. In four years of living near New York City, I had scarcely fished these waters, kept away by frequent overseas travel and a misguided conviction that any trout stream so close to Gotham had to be overrun with anglers and was not worth the trouble. But looking at the Beaverkill on a somber January afternoon I realized I had been wrong. I vowed to return in the spring, this time with a fly rod.

PELHAM, NEW YORK
APRIL, 1998

The Willowemoc meets the Beaverkill. This sentence—this unmistakably American lyric—fixes like coordinates the fountainhead of our fly fishing heritage.

Bradford Camps, Maine

Igor Sikorsky may have aviation in the genes but he has brook trout on the brain. Igor runs a traditional 19th-century sporting camp, Bradford Camps, in the North Maine Woods. The numerous lakes in this part of the state hold some of the largest brookies south of Labrador.

Roaring Branch, Vermont

Batten Kill, Vermont

The Delaware River is an exceptionally fine stretch of trout water. A big river, running through miles of inaccessible countryside and holding plentiful wild fish, the Delaware may well be the heavyweight champ of eastern fly fishing.

Fishing Creek, Clinton County, Pennsylvania

Following the lead of fly fishing's first author, Dame Juliana Berners (1496), more and more women are experiencing the pleasures of angling—"a merry occupation, without care, anxiety or trouble." This female sensibility has certainly enriched the sport, and contrary to quaint caricatures from the past, skillful women anglers are a common sight on today's trout streams.

Aroostook County, Maine

Falling Spring Branch, Pennsylvania

Roaring Branch, Vermont

Travelers from near and far flock to
Vermont to experience the glory of the fall
foliage. A lucky few view it from the
middle of a trout stream.

Batten Kill, Vermont

Ammonoosuc River, Vermont

It is said that King George's troops, having been routed, retreated across the river. They emerged

dripping on the far bank with their white pants turned yellow, and the name of one of

Pennsylvania's great spring creeks, the Yellow Breeches, was born.

East Branch Ausable River, New York

Upper Beaverkill River, New York

West Branch Ausable River, New York

LeTort Spring Run

For fabled flywater and
legendary anglers, Pennsylvania
is in a class by itself. The
LeTort, Yellow Breeches, Penns
Creek; George Harvey, Charlie
Fox, Joe Humphreys—these
names resonate at the heart of
American fly fishing.

Penns Creek

Indian River, New York

Most anglers believe that the West Branch of the Ausable in the Adirondack Mountains ranks among the finest trout streams in the East. Certainly it is among the most beautiful.

Sundown Creek, New York

Spring Creek, Pennsylvania

Reflecting the abundant sky, the rivers of the West tend to run blue. On the other hand, the intimate streams of the East often throw back the soft greens and yellows of the trees and shrubs lining their banks.

On the Margaree

GRANT McCLINTOCK

GLANCE out the Airstream window. Our trailer park neighbor is washing his bus. It was gleaming when he began. He soaps the rear tire in slow determined circles. If he backs up three steps, we'll be shaking hands in my kitchen.

I finish tying another fly. I'm a hamhanded beginner, but I've already created an impressive pile which looks to be a lifetime supply to me. This fly is called a green butt black bear—a purely descriptive name which feels like the last line of a beat poem. I sit back and stare into the middle distance for a moment. Annie Lenox slides through "A Whiter Shade of Pale." Perhaps one more green butt black bear—then, I think, a nap.

My oldest dog is already asleep at my feet—whimpering, dreaming. His legs twitch and rake the air. He's running down the cottontail which dares to dart across his dreamscape. Awake, the old boy can't get into the truck without help. Paula is off on a thirty-mile drive to buy a bag of mussels. They're so cheap here in Cape Breton. You could gravel a driveway with them for fifty bucks, but we'll eat ours tonight with garlic and butter. My neighbor straightens to admire his work. A soapy tire. He stares for a time, apparently seeing something I do not. He reaches for the

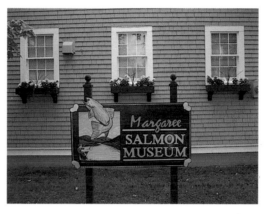

hose. One hand is cocked on his hip. A cigarette hangs from the center of his mouth. The smoke snakes lazily up his face. He squints, holding the hose over the tire. The suds slowly slip to the ground. Nothing is revealed, but that nap is now a dead certainty.

Paula, our three goldens and I have been living in the trailer for seven months now, 30,000 miles worth of this particular experience. Pulling out of our regular-life driveway for the last time those seven months ago, we were positively giddy with the success of our escape. That thrill seems as remote as grade school now. In pursuit, mundane reality has traveled quickly and caught us easily. Fibrous new routines, remarkably like those left behind, have shot up overnight. Life gets normal in a hurry. Trailer life has become everyday life, a fact at once comforting and unsettling.

Stays at trailer parks are measured in dog years—four days are a month, ten years and you're dead. Three weeks have passed since we arrived on the Margaree River—a long time in this Cape Breton trailer park. Old-timers can't remember when we arrived. I've begun thinking about running for school board.

We are falling behind schedule. The leaves are beginning to change in New England without us. The buck brookies down in

Maine are turning red as Creole tomatoes. Tomorrow I will photograph at Seal Pool, and the next morning I must leave, although I've been saying this for a couple of days now.

Back in home sweet Oklahoma, our gods would attend to this trailer park inertia by sweeping a couple of jumbo twisters through the area in the dead of night—Airstream accelerators, redneck relocators. Bewildered Okies would fly like confetti through the night air. In the morning they would awaken strewn through the branches of jack oaks and cottonwoods, scratch their heads, climb down and move on.

But this is Cape Breton where a man could wait a lifetime for a tornado to rearrange his life. Day after tomorrow, we're gone.

THREE WEEKS EARLIER, my first day on the Margaree.

I stand alone on the bank just above an enormous pool known as The Forks. A hundred yards upriver a lone angler is punching short, crisp casts into a narrow channel of pocket water. I have caught exactly one Atlantic salmon in my life. Nevertheless, I am prepared to assume the mantle of expert and declare that particular piece of water incapable of holding a salmon. I dismiss the upstream fisherman as a benighted novice, although I must admit he casts a very nice line.

Salmon fishing on the Margaree River offers a nice look at democracy in action. All mankind is invited to purchase the very reasonably priced license, head for the river and begin fishing. Quality salmon water does not get more public than this. No need to enter a drawing, often months in advance, for the right to wet a line. No need to hire a required-by-law guide principally distinguished in his ability to consume huge amounts of coffee from the seated position. On the Margaree the angler finds no posted stretches protecting the best spots for a select, lucky few. This river is a real free for all. As to access, the laws seem designed to make the salmon angling clan swoon with joy. The enlightened Nova Scotia legislature, apparently a gang of fly fishing Marxists, has decreed that any person carrying a fly rod be allowed to cross any piece of land in order to reach the river. The petit bourgeois concept of private property will not stay the proletarian fly fisher on his noble quest.

I am toting a camera and a couple of lenses. The light is flat, the water is low and few salmon are being caught on the Margaree River. A nasty drought grips Atlantic Canada. Without fresh water, few new salmon are coming into the Margaree, and the forecast calls for more dry weather. The gods conspire to ruin my life, but I take it like a man. I vow to return to the Airstream, crack open a jeroboam of Jim Beam, and indulge in thirty exhilarating minutes of blaming everything on my wife. I believe it was Camus who wrote that there are five stages of drunkenness, unless you live in a trailer park—then there are six.

I give the upstream fisherman a final perfunctory glance, and. . . hold on, what's this? He is crab-walking his way down the riffle water, inching toward the bank in my direction. He holds his fly rod in both hands high above his head. The rod bends towards the water in a tight trembling arc. Just as he reaches the bank at the head of the pool, a nice salmon decides to swap elements and heads for air. The fish snaps off a half twist and crashes back into the river dorsal first, a startling fan of white water shoots out flat over the calm, black pool. I summon what little agility has been granted me and hustle up the rocky bank. The salmon jumps two more times before I reach the angler, and now the fish is head down, plowing out deep runs.

"Mind if I take a couple of photos," I gasp. I have covered just seventy-five yards but look like a fellow who has completed

the Iron Man in neoprene waders. My face is, I am confident, purple.

"Ah, she's jumped out, eh. But, ya, shoot all you want." He is a handsome, lean man in his mid-thirties with angular features. His voice bounds along with the cheerful ups and downs of a Cape Breton accent.

The fish turns and bulls its way upriver, nose down. The fisherman adjusts the angle of the rod, takes a step back and raises the tip a touch higher. The adjustment takes hold, and the salmon's enthusiasm for the upriver run slackens.

After ten minutes, the salmon surfaces and enters the thrashing stage. The thick tail digs out great divots of water. Fury shoots up the fly line and down the bend of rod onto our angler who calmly absorbs and decodes it—a communiqué from the front. It must be hopeful news, for the battle, which to this point has been a back and forth affair, turns very one-sided, and the

Laurie MacDonald

angler begins to move the fish toward the shore with real purpose.

The salmon is mastered. I prepare myself for the obligatory fish-porn photograph. For this, the angler will generally plaster a jaw-numbing grin across his face and extend the fish as far as possible towards the camera. This provides the mixed blessing of rendering the fish larger than it really is but the fisherman smaller than he wants to be.

"Say when, eh." The angler holds the salmon by the tail in the shallow water, nose pointed upstream. The fish, a bright twelve-pounder, waves slowly back and forth like a heavy weed in a current.

"OK, lift her up," I say as I raise the camera.

On one knee, he sweeps the salmon from the water and strikes what I recognize as his signature pose. Rather than pushing the fish toward the camera, he cradles it just away from his chest, the salmon's head slightly to the left and the tail well to the right.

He looks not at the camera, but rather, with slightly bemused pride, down at the fish's head—the familiar new father's delivery room pose revisited.

"Ho, have a look at these lice, will ya?"

In very few circumstances would such an invitation generate enthusiasm. Salmon fishing, however, is the exception. Salmon anglers prize fish which have just reached the river from the salt—the more recent the arrival, the better. These fish have an overall silver tone, the protective coloration of choice in the open sea, and are referred to as "bright" or "fresh." Along with bright coloration, the presence of sea lice is a sure indication of a salmon's new arrival in the river. These lice attach to the salmon in the sea and enjoy a salmonid ocean voyage doing whatever it is lice do. Sea lice cannot live in fresh water so the joke's on them when the salmon enter the river. The lice die and drop off within a couple of days, providing an excellent barometer of how long a fish has been in fresh water. This measurement can be refined by observing whether or not the lice's tail is still attached—once again, a concern surely unique to salmon fishing. The tail apparently drops off first and quite quickly. The discover of lice with tails means a very recent arrival.

As the photo session ends, I move closer to quality-check the lice. They are lively all right, with tails aplenty whipping wildly in hope of jumping ship and hooking up with a badly needed salt fix.

The angler deftly plucks three or four lice from the salmon's back. Is he going to eat them? I am transfixed. No, instead, he pulls a small white card, folded in half, from his vest. He opens the card and brushes the lice onto it. They continue to wiggle but seem to sense that something has gone very wrong. Their enthusiasm is waning. Next to them on the card are several little groupings of the lice brethren, utterly desiccated and still. Now I understand. These are trophies.

"We all keep count on the river. Good to know where you stand, eh."

He holds the fish by the tail in the shallow water, nose upstream. Sensing the salmon has recovered, he releases the tail. The fish remains motionless, and for an odd moment we are all held together by something other than hook and line. A shutter moves down the fish's thick back. The tail folds once against the water, and the salmon slips out of sight toward the bottom of the pool.

The angler looks up at me. A smile widens across his face. The thin lipped Teutonic visage of a central casting Nazi lieutenant melts into a rather boyish grin of unmistakable warmth tinged with a mischievous ain't-life-odd hint of irony.

He folds the card and replaces it in his vest. He stands and extends his hand.

"Well, my name's Laurie MacDonald."

Meeting Laurie attached to an Atlantic salmon was a fortuitous and apt introduction, but as I learned over the next three weeks, not an altogether exceptional situation. Day after day, whether guiding or fishing alone, Laurie took salmon when others did not. With a degree of openness and generosity surprising to these jaded gringo eyes, Laurie took me under his wing and introduced me to the Margaree and many of the local anglers. It would be hard to overstate the friendliness of the reception. Time and again, I was made to feel not just a welcome visitor, but an expected guest.

THREE WEEKS PASS, and our last day in Cape Breton arrives. I have planned to spend it at Seal Pool which has become something of a second home for me.

I awaken too early and give myself a pre-dawn haircut. I hold up a mirror to trim the back. The reflection fools me every time. I cannot be trained. I reach left, but the hand in the mirror goes right. Undaunted, I clip away. When I'm done, it looks bad, very bad. Just above my left ear, a square chunk of hair the size of a peach pit has disappeared. How did that happen? I check the nape of my neck with the mirror. The hairline jitterbugs aimlessly. This is worse than a head shot. If I have a stroke today, I'll need a closed casket.

Paula and the dogs, piled together on the bed, breath heavily in and out as one unit. I consider waking her for a bit of sympathy but think better of it. I take my bad haircut, throw on a jacket and slip out the door.

The truck door slams shut, a mortar shot against the morning stillness. Unnoticed in the night, a heavy fog has eased down upon us. A good morning for shooting, I think. I drive slowly up the dirt road toward the highway. The trailer park's miniature golf course sits muted in the fog—worn out pinks and greens. A little lighthouse blocks the approach to the third hole.

I have a twenty minute drive to Seal Pool. I switch on CBC, the affable Canadian public radio network. The CBC chirps away—cheerful, lighthearted, unfettered. Lots of Celtic music, townhall reports, cozy eccentric tales from the Yukon, quaint radio dramas. They speak of America often with a mix of concern and befuddlement. It's an overly spicy stew south of the border—too much passion, too many guns.

I park beside the highway behind Laurie's car. The fog to the east is beginning to glow. The sun is creeping into place.

I trudge across an open field weighed down with all the knickknacks of both fly fishing and photography: lenses, fly boxes, film, filters, clippers, fly rod, cameras, bug dope, tripod. In a better world all of this would be in hands of nubile assistants, understudies who worship the master and happily trail behind burdened with his gear, safari style. I would enter the playing field as unencumbered as royalty.

I arrive at a familiar bend in the river. Seal Pool stretches straight away from me for a hundred yards before vanishing into the fog. I can see a half dozen anglers. Arms lift and fall. Fly lines slowly unfold in rhythmic waves and straighten out over the river, as if only lightly touched by some languid lunar gravity.

Down the pool, deeper into the fog the fishermen are phantoms, more movement than form. Their bright lines occasionally blink orange or yellow as they cut heavy air, catching the light for a moment before becoming once again invisible.

I set up the tripod and attach a telephoto lens. Through the viewfinder the world is suddenly compressed, space deleted. The landscape is drawn to me like an accordion closing. Through the lens I recognize the man at the head of the pool, Bill Chaisson. Laurie introduced him as Willie Joe. He is eighty-four, throws a beautiful tight line and catches plenty of salmon—a fixture on the Margaree, a respected man. He carries a Thermos of tea and bag of cookies to the river, more to share than to consume. I found myself sitting on the Seal Pool bench with Willie Joe a couple of times, sipping his tea and munching his cookies.

"What fly'd you use, Bill?" I asked one day, gazing down at the grilse he had landed fifteen minutes ago. It lay motionless in the grass by the bench, more forlorn than majestic at this point.

He reached around, grabbed his rod and showed me the fly.

"Huh, that's an Adams," I said.

"Oh, you know your flies, don't you?"

Naming the Adams, most common of North American trout flies, was an accomplishment on a par with identifying the moon in the evening sky.

"I didn't know people used the Adams for salmon, Bill."

"Yeah, I do like it. I tie it on a salmon hook, of course." He stretches the Adams to arms length where it finally falls into focus for his octogenarian eyes. He admires it for a moment. "Hey, what do *you* think might work today?"

These well-mannered Cape Bretoners want to include everyone in the fun, so like their jolly Cajun brethren in far-off Louisiana.

"I got no idea, Bill. I've only caught one salmon in my life."

"Have another cookie."

He is a big man whose powerful body belies his eighty-four years. He is endlessly cheerful, generous with his knowledge. Willie Joe positively glows with good will.

Next angler down the pool is Laurie. He's fishing a dry fly, shooting a reach-cast to the far bank. I linger here. I love watching Laurie fish. When he enters the river, he drops comfortably into the moment and remains securely anchored there for hours on end. Years ago as a young man, Laurie wandered in the desert of obsession—a nervous land where one takes fish like drugs, where everything from the death of Mother Teresa to the tide is somehow about catching salmon. He now lands more fish than ever, but the sense of feverish pursuit is gone. The salmon now seem to pursue *him*. It is all process at this point. He seeks the perfect parachute cast, the flawless turle knot, ultimate drag-free drift—a circular journey of small, unhurried steps occasionally interrupted by a salmon. The universe cartwheels; Laurie goes fishing.

Beyond Laurie are two fellows I haven't seen before.

Unbelievable casters. Tight loops way out over the water. These are definitely sports, impeccably dressed. The one closest to me is tall and thin. He wears those new oval, wrap-around sun glasses which make him look like a dragonfly in a ball cap. The second sport is shorter, stocky with neither glasses not hat. Even buffered by a 300mm lens, I sense a hint of pent-up aggression in his bullet casts.

On the far high bank in the fog I can just make out an angler casting a two-handed rod. From his stand above the river, his line sails out—impossible distances that suggest some sleight of hand. That would be Henry Green from Virginia, a tidy man with a neat white mustache, a compact version of a Hemingway. His energy is palpable, bright in his eyes. Henry took early retirement from the Civil Service at the end of Jimmy Carter's run. His friends warned, "You'll get bored soon enough."

"Watch me," he answered.

He salmon fishes in Cape Breton and Newfoundland. He hunts grouse daily on Virginia mountain tops during their season. He's an enthusiastic and skilled birder. An amateur naturalist. An animated conversationalist. He strikes me as an American sportsman of the best sort, full of life-embracing enthusiasm, anything but bored.

A week earlier I was standing by Henry as he fished the high bank. From somewhere in the distance came a faint, plaintive cry. "Hello. Hello."

The voice seemed to be coming from the throat of a distressed child abandoned in the high branches of an evergreen downstream.

"What the hell is that?" I asked Henry.

"I've been hearing it for a few days. Probably somebody's pet crow that got lost."

Bill Chaisson

"Crows can talk?"

"Sometimes. If you split their tongues."

I am left to ponder this in silence for a moment.

"Hello. Hello."

"Eerie, isn't it?" said Henry as he delivered another hundred feet of fly line out over the river.

I EXPOSE thirty or forty transparencies, one of which will eventually crawl from the dismal swamp of the editing table to perch in this book.

Fishermen and photographers, alike in many ways. From experience each learns to accept and eventually embrace the profundity of chance. Our rewards are dealt out with devine randomness. We may try to bend the odds our way by fishing the right fly or being in the right position to shoot a forming rainbow, but in the end, a great fish or a memorable photograph is a gift.

ALBERT JENKINS worries a spool of six-pound test through his fingers, turning it over and over like a silver dollar. He is guiding the two previously mentioned sports today and has been for the last three days. The sports are a couple of young Germans who understand a thing or two about fly fishing. They have hired Albert to lead them to the pool and then disappear. They know how to catch fish. The problem is that they are not catching any fish, and this disturbs Albert deeply.

He turns to me. "What do you think?"

"About what, Albert?"

"Oh, the leader, eh. They're on eight pound. That's too heavy for this water. Should be down to six or even five by now, don't you think?"

"Tell 'em."

"I did, you know, but they ah. . . won't listen. Maybe they're right, but I don't think so. This water is awful thin." He pauses and stares out at his charges for a moment.

"They can sure cast though."

Hard to put a number on Albert's age. Somewhere in my range, much older than the Germans. I've never seen him fish, but Laurie says he's one of the finest guides on the river.

He looks up at me. "And I've got to say, I don't much like the way they're drifting that fly. It barely touches the water before they pick it up."

I had noticed that. It's a good idea to give the fish at least a chance to eat the fly.

"Albert, I think what these guys really like is casting."

"Oh, they're good casters all right. They should be taking fish."

Henry Green

This is killing him.

I rise from the bench and stretch. The fog has long since burned off. It is a lazy fall day. "I'm going to fish for awhile," I announce.

"Yeah, good idea. What are you going to try?"

I pluck a huge dry fly from my vest patch. It's a familiar salmon pattern known as a bomber. On the Margaree it is simply referred to as a bug. This one is light brown with a single white calf hair horn. Its arrival seems to add to Albert's distress.

"Thought I give this one a try," holding it up for Albert. "Laurie tied it. He's been using one."

Albert looks relieved. "Ah, well you'll be all right then,"

He gazes out at the Germans. They are whipping up the air in earnest.

"Hey, Albert, what can you do? Don't worry."

"They've fished all over the world, you know."

"I bet."

EIGHT SALMON WERE HOOKED AT SEAL POOL that day. Laurie and Henry landed two each, Willie Joe took one, a couple of visitors from the states caught one each, and I got one. Albert, who tailed it for me, said, "Twelve, maybe fourteen pounds," placing the bragging weight at fourteen pounds, minimum.

I had wandered down beyond the pool and had cast Laurie's bomber not twenty times before the salmon took the fly. She rose like a spring creek trout on a mayfly, dimpled the water and slipped off. The line went tight, and I put a good hook-set into her. She jumped four times—twice in locations which had little relationship to the direction of my line. She jumped for the last time toward the end of the fight, very close in. "That's unusual," said Albert at my elbow.

I managed to bring the fish to hand in respectable, if not spectacular, style. I had not committed some stupidity and lost the fish nor had I disgraced the family name by letting it swim around the pool unchallenged for half an hour.

Albert Jenkins

DEPARTURE DAY. We are rejuvenated—charmed gypsies moving our home about willy-nilly, a thrill very like the childhood naughtiness of skipping school.

I have detached the hoses, raised the awning, attached chains and sway bars. The Airstream and Suburban are once again mated. I sit sipping coffee at the picnic table just outside the trailer. The table is of an old style once endemic at public parks—made all of wood with crossed legs at either end, attached benches, painted dark red. These days one more often sees the heavier metal or concrete tables, usually chained to something. As we creep toward the millennium, more and more of the world must be nailed down.

I can hear Paula at work inside the Airstream. Before we set off, our little world must be nailed down too—the law of gravity supplemented with the twin theorems of bungee and Velcro.

Where do we need to be this evening? Who do I need to phone today? My mind slips from topic to topic until it stumbles across my salmon of yesterday, and there it settles like a sofa slug. The poet measures out his life in coffee spoons; we anglers use fish. In our heads swim the multitude we have hooked and landed over the years. Many, obscure in their insignificance, never surface, but the great ones—the memorable ones—are always close at hand, ready to dart into our consciousness. It is a memory more visceral than visual. We attempt to give form to this memory through measurement, length and weight. These bloodless sums are handy to spew out over cocktails if the talk turns to fish, but they fail to resurrect the essence of the beast. What numbers will we use to encompass that startling, pristine wildness—the swimming nerve of nature—which with rod and line we touch in passing? Will we discover the weight of the man or the sense of the moment hidden in the length of the fish? Suffice it to say that when the right fish and the right fisherman get together, the connection is complex and oddly intimate, at once humbling the ego and expanding the soul. It's a small thing to catch a fish, but sometimes it feels like the crux of the matter, like the pulse.

WE TOP A RISE and leave the Margaree Valley behind. We've been riding silently for thirty minutes, tossing our thoughts about in private. I want to say something memorable, but I don't know what. So like a bum who has stumbled into the lobby of the Waldorf, I blurt out, "I could live here."

Paula says, "So could I."

SEDONA, ARIZONA
APRIL, 1998

Seal Pool, Margaree River

In the minds of many anglers, no river is more closely associated with Atlantic salmon fishing than the Miramichi. This river combines a fine run of big fish, a dramatically beautiful setting and a history of fly fishing which goes back generations.

Miramichi River at Pond's upstream camp.

Pools in the wading section of the Grande Cascapédia are doled out by lottery. Two days in advance, names are drawn from a hat and pools assigned, adding a touch of Las Vegas excitement to this world-class salmon river on the Gaspé peninsula.

Grande Cascapédia

Dawn is the angler's first tee. Before him lies only possibility. He wades into the landscape of big fish where neither wind knot nor line-drag has yet intruded, where the future holds nothing but impeccable casting followed by heroic battles between fish and man. Then at dusk, he leaves the river, tempered by reality. But whether he's landed the fish of a lifetime or fallen in the water and filled his waders, there's always dawn tomorrow, and with it the chance to confirm or redefine everything.

Margaree River

Miramichi River

Salmon fishing requires patience—sometimes a lot of patience. Hours, days, even weeks can pass without the hint of a fish. Concentration becomes a task. Eventually you drop into a daze, taking comfort in the salmon angler's mantra—cast. . . step; cast. . . step. . . but then quite suddenly, and usually quite unexpectedly, you find yourself attached to that salmon sailing through the air. At that point, concentration ceases to be an issue.

Miramichi River

Margaree River

Matapédia

Miramichi River

The Forks, Margaree River

It is doubtful that you will ever have
the Forks Pool on the Margaree to
yourself and equally doubtful that
you will ever fish in more congenial
company.

Most of us clean our fly lines once a year at the beginning of the season, if that. Salmon anglers, always looking for that slightly longer cast, tend to be a bit more fastidious and arrive at the river prepared for a little on-stream cleaning whenever the need arises.

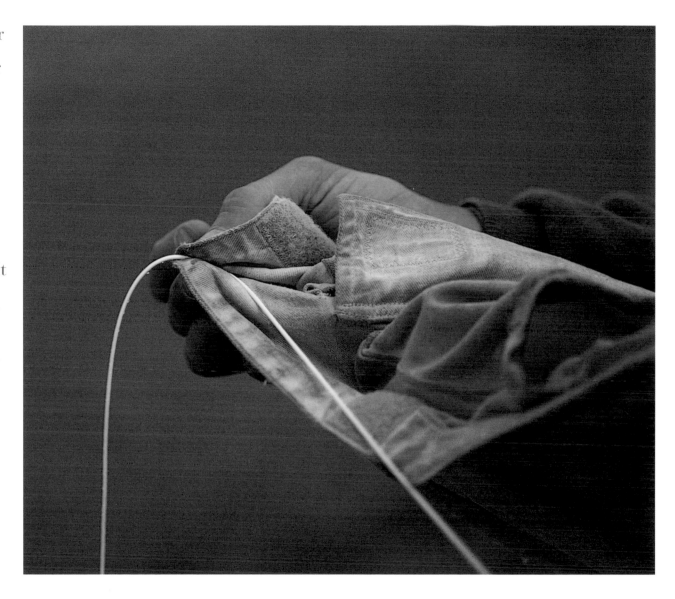

You have just spent an hour carefully fishing your way down one of the Bonaventure's astonishing emerald green pools—never moved a fish. As you wade back to the beach, two québécois anglers enter the water. One carries a large box, a home-made periscope designed for under water viewing. In a welcome nod to bilingualism, this fish finder is known as a look-à-tous. The first angler plunges the box into the water. He rotates the look-a-tous slowly back and forth, scrupulously surveying the contents of the pool. After a couple of minutes of this, he raises his head, turns to his pal and announces, "Vide. Allons." (Empty. Let's go.) And they're off to the next spot.

Margaree River

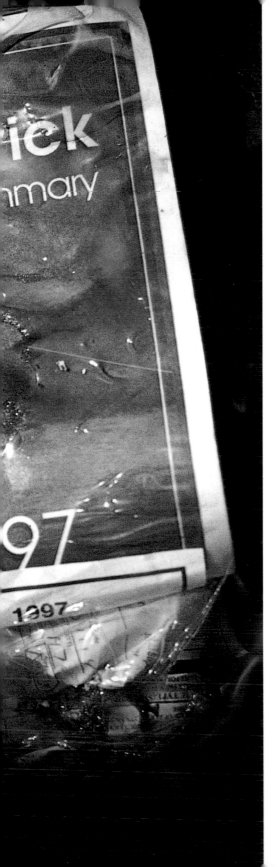

The year ends. Licenses and regulations are tossed on the campfire with poignant regret. The past season is relegated to memory, a river flowing backward into fog, and the coming season lies far ahead in the treacherous land of hopes and dreams. The off-season has arrived—the time to reflect and recompose the past, to plan and construct the future. The dual reality of the angler—a way of life like any other—thought and action, fire and ice.

THANKS TO

Henry Williamson	Roger Lowe	Eddie Rogers	Bill Hamill
Michael Blakely	Ryan Hodges	John MacDonald	Andy Knorr
Jerome Alexandre	Jason Woods	Keith Pond	Paula McClintock
Karen Waldron	Creed Taylor	Brad Pond	Leita Hamill
Bo Aughtry	Dan Shields	Igor & Karen Sikorsky	Walker Blanton
Ben Willingham	Rachel Finn	Gary Corson	Kirk VanValkenburgh
Jim Woltz	Jerry Bottcher	Laurie MacDonald	Nick Lyons
Jeff Clark	Sam Lambert	Bob Mead	Carol Haralson
Byron Begley	David Hoag	Fen Montaigne	
Ronnie Hall	Alan Kitz	Jody Parker	

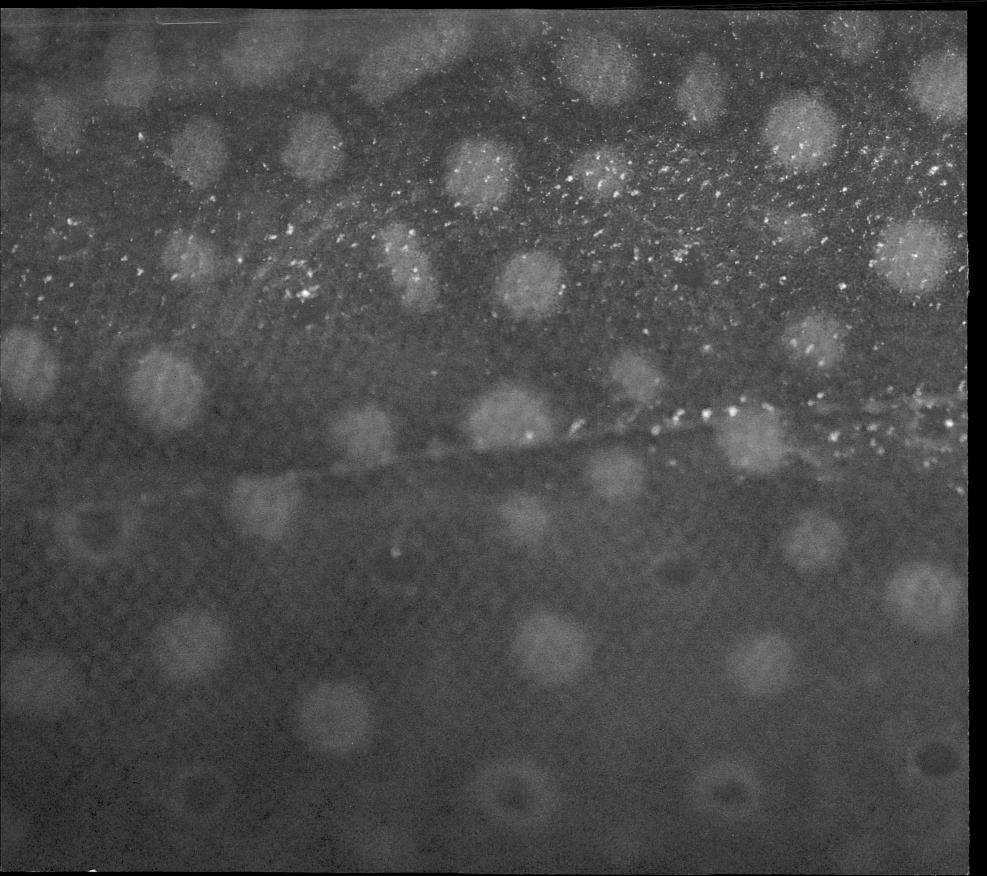